Danae Dobson
and Dr. James Dobson

Parables for Kids

*Eight contemporary
stories based on
best-loved
Bible parables*

Illustrated by Carolyn Ewing

TYNDALE
KIDS

Tyndale House Publishers, Inc.
Wheaton, Illinois

Visit Tyndale's exciting Web site at www.tyndale.com

Illustrated by Carolyn Ewing

Edited by Betty Free

Designed by Beth Sparkman

Library of Congress Cataloging-in-Publication Data

Dobson, Danae.
   Parables for kids / Danae Dobson, James Dobson.
     p.   cm.
     Summary: Retells eight parables, such as the Prodigal Son, the
Persistent Widow, and the Good Samaritan, in terms of modern
situations. Includes the Biblical version and interpretive text.
    ISBN 0-8423-0637-4 (alk. paper)
    1. Jesus Christ—Parables—Juvenile literature.   [1. Jesus
Christ—Parables. 2. Parables. 3. Bible stories—N.T.]
  I. Dobson, James C., date. II. Title
  BT376.D63 1999
  242'.62—dc21   98-33381

Printed in the United States of America

05   04   03   02   01   00   99
7   6   5   4   3

CONTENTS

For my dad,
who is a constant
source of support
and encouragement
in my life.
Thank you
for giving your time
to this project.
I love you.
Danae

What You Should Know

You're going to learn in this book about the parables of Jesus, which are stories that teach us about God. Understanding these truths from the Bible will help you to be happy and please God. But sometimes the parables need to be explained. That is why my daughter, Danae, has written eight interesting stories that are based on the words of Jesus. They might even remind you of members of your own family. After you have read these fun stories, I will explain the parables of Jesus.

Let me start with this important idea. Most people think a lot about themselves. They may be selfish, greedy, and uncaring toward others. But that isn't what the Bible teaches. Jesus talked about something he called "the kingdom of God." The parables help us understand this kingdom—this better way. They teach us to be unselfish, forgiving, and kind, and to do other things that God would have us to do.

You will learn about this wonderful kingdom that Jesus spoke about when you read Danae's stories and my explanations of the parables. Maybe you will write Danae and me after you've read our book. I hope so.

James Dobson

The Runaway

Based on the Parable of the Prodigal Son

LUKE 15:11-32

lam!

The bedroom door closed with a loud boom.

Michael Healy threw himself on the bed and buried his face in a pillow.

"I can't take it anymore!" he said out loud. "I've got to get out of here!" His breath felt hot as he breathed in and out of the cotton pillowcase.

Rolling onto his back, Michael stared at the ceiling, where a poster of *Jurassic Park* hung over his head. He crossed his arms and thought about what had just taken place with his father.

It began as a beautiful Saturday, and twelve-year-old Michael planned to go bowling with his friends. But when his dad found out chores and homework weren't finished, he forbade Michael to go. An argument started, and before long Michael broke one of the rules by raising his voice. He was instantly grounded and told to go to his room—for the *second* time in one week!

Michael felt trapped as he lay on the bed, staring at the ceiling. He took his stereo remote off the nightstand and clicked the power button. None of the music interested him. He turned it off and let out a deep sigh.

Dad doesn't want me to have any fun, he said to himself. *He won't let me grow up—he tries to be cruel.*

Michael knew in his heart those things weren't true. He knew his parents loved him and his sister more than anything. But Michael was angry, and he was thinking things he didn't really mean. Michael was also about to do something he would later regret.

Michael pushed himself off the bed and went over to the closet. When he opened it, at least ten shoes and a basketball tumbled out. What a mess! He reached for his camouflage army tote bag and flung it on the bed.

I'm getting out of here, he thought, *even if I have to run away!*

Michael began pulling clothes out of the drawer and stuffing them into his bag. He loosened his allowance from a money clip and counted twenty-seven dollars.

That's enough to last for a while, he said to himself, cramming it down the pocket of his jeans.

Michael grabbed his bus pass and took one last look around the room. Then he crammed a Chicago Bears cap on his head and unlocked the window. He was just about to swing one leg over the ledge when his bedroom door opened. It was his sister, Amy. For a seven-year-old she could sure be a pest!

"Didn't I tell you to knock first?" Michael snapped.

"I'm sorry," Amy apologized. She was popping purple bubble gum through her teeth.

"Wha'cha doing?" she asked.

"Shh!" said Michael. He put his finger to his lips. "Be quiet. I don't want Mom and Dad to know."

"Know what?" asked Amy.

Michael walked over to where she was standing and put his hands on her shoulders. "I'm running away," he whispered.

Amy's mouth opened so wide her gum fell out. "Ooh, you're going to get in a lot of trouble," she warned.

"No I won't, 'cuz I'm not going to be here," said Michael. "Now keep quiet!"

He went back to the window and threw his tote bag over the ledge.

Amy seemed at a loss for words, almost as if she were in shock. "Wh-when are you coming back?" she asked.

Michael shrugged. "I don't know. Maybe never. I have to get out of here so I can run my own life. I'm tired of being told what to do, and I'm sick of being grounded. Dad and I aren't getting along, so maybe it's best if I just leave."

Michael thought he saw a tear in his sister's eye, but he chose to ignore it. This was no time to get emotional!

With one giant leap Michael was out the window and running across the yard. The boy looked back and glanced at his sister one more time. Amy stood at the win-dow with her hands against the glass, looking sad and confused.

Michael felt a lump in his throat but quickly dismissed it. *There's no turning back now,* he thought. *This is it!*

Michael rode a bus downtown and got off in front of the bowling alley. He was hoping his pals would be there so they could play a few games.

When he entered the building, his mood suddenly changed—his friends were nowhere to be seen.

Oh, well, Michael said to himself, *I can still have a good time.*

He walked over to the counter and plunked down seven dollars. "Two games, please," he said.

"Do you need bowling shoes?" asked the attendant.

Michael nodded.

"That's another three dollars."

He paid the fee and headed to lane 11.

Michael bowled well and even made a few strikes, but it wasn't much fun by himself. He noticed a lot of people were staring at him too. Some of the men looked pretty rough with their cigars and bottles of beer. It made Michael want to get out of there fast.

He stood in front of the bowling alley and looked up and down the street. Suddenly he felt a wave of excitement. He was free! No chores, no homework, no responsibilities. He could go anywhere he wanted and do anything he pleased. There was no one standing in his way. It was almost too good to be true.

Michael spotted a theater where the latest Muppet movie was playing. He hurried to the box office and checked the time—perfect! The show was starting in ten minutes. He bought a ticket and a tub of popcorn and sat down in the middle section.

As the lights dimmed, Michael couldn't help but think of his dad for a moment. After all, his father had taken him to earlier Muppet films when Michael was younger. Somehow it didn't seem right that his dad wasn't sitting next to him. It made Michael feel a little sad, but by the time the coming attractions flashed on the screen, he'd forgotten all about it.

When the film was over, Michael walked to Burger King and ordered some food. He sat outside at a picnic table and watched the cars rush by.

Everybody is in such a hurry, Michael thought. *I wish I had somewhere important to go.*

He pulled the pickles out of his Whopper and threw them in the trash.

By now it was getting late. *What am I doing here at night by myself?* Michael wondered, taking a bite of his sandwich. *I wanted to run away, but I sure didn't plan very well. It's cold, and I've got nowhere to go, no place to sleep, and I'm down to . . .*

Michael reached into his pocket.

Two bucks! That isn't going to get me very far.

Michael sighed and looked at his food. Suddenly he wasn't hungry anymore. He threw his half-eaten burger away and slung his tote bag over his shoulder.

I don't know where I'm going, but I've got to keep moving, he said to himself.

Michael checked his watch—11:00 P.M. He was starting to feel tired as he made his way along the dark street. He thought of his warm bed at home, with the down comforter and fluffy pillows. For the first time, no one was making him go to bed, and yet that was exactly what he wanted to do.

Some homeless people were gathered in a nearby alley.

"Hey, kid!" someone yelled. "Come here! What's your name?"

Michael quickened his pace.

It seemed as if he'd walked for miles when he came to an Amtrak sign. He remembered seeing movies where people slept in train stations.

Maybe I can spend the night here, he thought.

Michael entered the building and looked around. Sure enough, a few people were sprawled out on chairs, fast asleep. Most of them looked homeless, and one man appeared to be drunk.

Michael lay down on two plastic seats, using his tote bag for a pillow. The chairs were hard and uncomfortable.

Am I going to have to sleep here from now on? he wondered.

Michael swallowed hard as a tear ran down his cheek. He thought of his dad and mom and even his pesky sister, Amy. He was starting to really miss them.

"Leaving home was a stupid thing to do," Michael whispered. "Now I'll never see my family again."

He rubbed his nose. "It's too late to go back now," he sniffed. "They probably wouldn't want me anyway."

Michael folded his arms and curled up on the two chairs. Then he fell asleep.

"Are you all right, kid? Do you need help?"

Michael awoke to see a middle-aged man standing over him. His uniform showed he worked for the railroad company.

Michael sat up and rubbed his eyes.

"I'm OK," he lied. "I was just leaving."

The man looked concerned as Michael grabbed his tote bag and headed out the door.

The sun was coming up, and it hurt his eyes. He felt groggy from having just awakened. *Where do I go now?* the boy thought to himself.

Michael went into a deli and spent his last two dollars on juice and a cold roll.

He remembered his mother's cooking as he walked along the street. The pancakes, the sausage—how good those would taste right now.

A man on the corner was holding a Will Work for Food sign. Michael had a new appreciation for people like that—now he knew how they felt.

He kicked an empty Coke can along the sidewalk. All of a sudden a new thought occurred to him. *If I promise Dad I'll work hard every week doing chores, he might let me come back. Maybe I can go home!*

The boy began running toward the bus stop.

Why didn't I think of this sooner? he wondered as he took a window seat. He pressed his nose against the glass and thought about what he might say to his dad.

Michael's palms were sweaty, and his heart was thumping fast. By the time the bus reached his street, his legs felt as if they weighed two hundred pounds!

Michael rehearsed his story as he began walking toward his house. In the distance he could see a crowd of people standing in his front yard.

What's going on? he wondered.

He took a deep breath and forced himself to keep walking. When he got closer to his home, he saw that the people in the yard were neighbors. His mother and father were there too. They had their arms around each other, and it looked as if his mom had been crying.

Michael stopped walking and hung his head. He was too ashamed to speak or even look up.

Then he heard his father call out his name! His dad ran toward him and, in no time at all, threw his strong arms around his boy.

"Michael! Son! You're safe!"

Michael closed his eyes and buried his face in his father's chest. Tears streaked down his dirty cheeks.

"I'm sorry, Dad," he mumbled. It was all he could say.

When a hand touched his shoulder, Michael looked up to see his mother standing over him. She wiped her eyes and kissed him on the forehead. "I was so worried," she said. "The neighbors organized a search party to try to find you— that's why they're here."

Just then Michael felt someone grab him around the waist. It was Amy! She gave him the biggest bear hug her sixty-pound body could offer. "I missed you," she said.

Michael had never been so happy to see his family!

"Is it OK for me to come home?" he asked.

"What you did was wrong," said his father. "But I think you know that. We'll talk about it later. For now, let's celebrate with our friends."

"I'll make your favorite meal—homemade pizza," said his mother.

Michael swallowed hard. "I-I don't deserve a party," he said. "I was hoping you'd let me come back if I promised to work and—"

"Michael, we're just glad that you're alive!" said his father. "We were so concerned about you. But now you're home, and you're safe—that's why I want to celebrate."

Michael choked back the tears as he looked up at his dad's face. "I love you," he whispered.

"I love you, too," said his father. "More than you'll ever know."

One by one the neighbors came to hug Michael and welcome him back. Between hugs, he glanced at his dad and smiled. It sure felt good to be home again!

The Parable of the Prodigal Son

LUKE 15:11-32

What you just read was a story about a boy who ran away from home. It was based on a parable told by Jesus in the book of Luke. The young man was older than Michael, maybe 20 years of age, and he probably got tired of his parents telling him what to do. He hated working on the family farm with his father and brother. As he sweat in the fields each day, he began thinking about how much he would like to get away. Finally he asked for money from his father and left home. It was a very selfish thing to do.

The young man went to live in a faraway city, where he began doing wrong things. He also began wasting his money. That is why he is sometimes called the *Prodigal Son,* which means "a young man who spends his money foolishly."

You can guess what happens to people who live like that. They usually go broke, just like Michael did in *our* story. That's when the fun stops. Even their friends don't want to be around them anymore.

The Prodigal Son soon found himself in a lot of trouble. There wasn't enough food for the people at that time, and the young man got very hungry. He became homeless and desperate. The only job he could find was taking care of pigs, and even the slop they were eating looked good to him. He was starving to death. That's when he realized he had done something really stupid! He began thinking about his dad, who had been so good to him. Maybe his father would give him a job on the farm—not as a son but as a worker who would not get paid. He began the long journey home to ask his father to forgive him for his great sin. But when his father saw him coming down the road, he ran and threw his arms around the boy. The father held a great feast and took the young man back, not just as a worker, but as the son he greatly loved.

Each of Jesus' parables teaches us something important. What do you think he is telling us about in the story of the Prodigal Son? Jesus wants us to understand that sin is a terrible thing. It always causes people to feel pain and sorrow. If you disobey God's teachings in the Bible, sin will cause hurt in your life too. But this parable also tells us something else. The father in the story is like God. Jesus wants us to know that God loves us even when we are doing things that are wrong. Our heavenly Father is always ready to forgive us when we turn from our sinful ways. He will welcome us home—not as an unpaid worker but as a member of his own family. More than anything else, Jesus' parable about the Prodigal Son tells us about the great love of God for his children.

And guess what? That includes you! He loves you very much!

JCD

An Answer Worth Waiting For

Based on the Parable of the Persistent Widow

LUKE 18:1-8

he aroma of freshly baked pretzels filled the air.

"One sugar-coated and a lemonade, please," said Rachel, placing three dollars on the counter. She turned to the girl standing beside her.

"What'll you have, Tori?"

"Just a plain one," answered her friend, fumbling in her purse for her wallet. She glanced at her big sister, who was sitting on a nearby bench waiting for them.

"Want a pretzel, Andrea?"

"No, thanks," replied the older girl.

Rachel and Tori munched on their snacks as they walked around the shopping center with Andrea. One of their favorite activities on Saturday was hanging out at the mall. They loved to shop, eat, and sometimes take in a movie. It made them feel grown up and important.

"Look at those sunglasses!" exclaimed Tori, hurrying to a store window. "They're Ray•Bans! Aren't they cool?"

Rachel bent down to get a closer look.

"They aren't my style, but they'd look good on you. Are you going to buy them?"

"Can't right now," Tori sighed. "Maybe I'll ask for them for my birthday." She bit into her pretzel and tore off a piece.

Tori's sister smiled and walked to another display window.

"I had that dream again last night," said Rachel.

"The one about your dad?" asked Tori.

"Yeah. It's been five years since he died, but I still feel really sad sometimes."

"That's normal," said Tori. She chewed and swallowed. "Just give it time."

"I've tried," said Rachel. "But it never gets any easier. I keep praying that someone will come and, you know, be kind of like a father. No one could take the place of my real dad, but I keep asking God to send *somebody*. Mom and I need someone to fix stuff and take us camping—things like that."

Tori looked up and rolled her eyes.

"Rachel, *come on!* You've been praying that silly prayer forever, and nothing has

changed. You're ten years old! It's time to grow up and accept things the way they are." Tori wadded up her pretzel wrapper and threw it in the trash.

Rachel felt a surge of anger, almost as if she'd been slapped in the face. Tori was a good friend, but she often said whatever came to mind without thinking. She was too outspoken and not at all sensitive to people's feelings. Sometimes Rachel let her get away with it, but not today!

"Just a minute, Tori," she snapped. "Who gave you the right to tell me to give up hope? I believe a miracle can happen no matter how long it takes. Besides, we learned in Sunday school that Jesus taught us to *never* doubt that he hears our prayers. You either weren't there, or you weren't listening that day!"

"I'm sorry, Rae," Tori said. "It's just that I don't like seeing you waste your time on a fantasy."

"I'm not wasting time," said Rachel assuredly. "Just because I keep praying for something doesn't mean I don't have a life."

"I know, I know," said Tori. "Let's drop it. I don't want to argue anymore."

Rachel agreed, but she was still irritated at her friend. What would Tori know about prayer anyway? She didn't even go to church very often.

After trying on silly hats and holding bunnies in the pet store, the girls grew tired of the mall. They rode their bikes home and parted ways at the intersection.

"Will you be at church tomorrow?" asked Rachel.

"Maybe," said Tori, pedaling down the street behind her sister.

"That probably means no," Rachel mumbled.

She arrived home to find her mother getting dressed for the evening.

"Where are you going?" she asked.

Her mother smiled. She had a sparkle in her eye that Rachel hadn't seen for a long time—not since before her father passed away.

"Remember that man I told you about?" asked her mother.

"Bob?"

"Yes! Well, he's taking me to dinner and the theater tonight. Do I look OK?" She turned toward the mirror and smoothed her dress.

"You look great, Mom," said Rachel.

"Grandma will be here in a minute," said her mother. "And your dinner is in the microwave. All you have to do is heat it up."

"OK," said Rachel. She went to the kitchen and set the timer on the microwave. Then she leaned on the counter and stared out the window.

I wish Dad were here so Mom wouldn't go out with someone else, she thought. *Bob sounds like a bore. He's a junior high teacher who's never been married and likes to go to*

dumb places like the theater. That's all I know about him. Oh well, if he makes Mom happy, I guess he's OK. Maybe I'm just being selfish.

She took her dinner out of the microwave. As she thanked God for the food, Rachel prayed again for a father. "Please, God, send someone who will be just like my dad." Then Rachel flipped on the TV. *Gilligan's Island* was on.

Pretty soon Mother walked in with her date. She was holding a big bouquet of flowers.

"Honey, I'd like you to meet Bob," she said.

Rachel glanced up from the television and lifted her hand. "Hi," she said.

"It's nice to meet you, Rachel," said Bob, grinning. "I've heard so much about you."

Rachel smiled. She wanted to say, "How original!" Instead she said, "Thanks. Have a good time tonight."

"We will," said Bob. He looked at her mother with that silly grin again.

Rachel sighed and turned her attention back to the TV.

■ ■ ■

That first night with Bob was just the beginning. It seemed every time Rachel turned around, there was Bob. Always taking her mother out, bringing something by, or helping around the house. It was nice of him to fix the leaky faucet and the VCR, but Rachel was starting to tire of his being there. She missed the days when she and her mom were alone. After all, they had a life before *he* came into the picture. Bob was always friendly to Rachel, but she only tolerated him. She didn't like it when her mother spent time with someone other than her dad, even though she really did want another father. Besides, Bob wasn't who she had in mind—after all, he didn't even like to go camping.

One Saturday Rachel was doing homework when the doorbell rang. When she opened the door, there stood Bob, holding two sacks of Chinese food.

"Hi," he said cheerfully. "I was in the area and thought I'd bring lunch over."

"Come on in," Rachel said, motioning toward the kitchen.

Bob waved to Rachel's mother, who was vacuuming the living-room carpet. Then he glanced at the papers spread all over the table.

"What are you doing?" he asked.

"Lots of stuff," Rachel answered. "I've got a test Monday, a book report to finish, and tons of math homework."

Bob pulled up a chair.

"Maybe I can help," he said.

"That's OK," said Rachel. "You don't have to."

"I want to," he said.

He was leaning down so he could see her face. Rachel noticed his eyes were kind and trusting. There was a certain sparkle that reminded her of her father— the way he used to look at her when he told bedtime stories.

"Are you sure?" she asked timidly.

"Absolutely," said Bob. "Put me to work!"

"Well, OK," said Rachel. "I guess I could use some help with math. It's never been my best subject, and we're learning new stuff right now."

For the next half hour Bob explained math problems and guided her along. Then he helped make a cover for her book report. They designed it in the shape of Texas since that was the subject of the book.

"It's perfect!" Rachel squealed. "I'll have the best-looking report in my class!"

Her mother came into the kitchen and pointed to the sacks of cold Chinese food on the counter.

"I'm hungry," she said. "Aren't you two going to stop long enough to eat?"

"Oh, yeah," laughed Rachel. "I guess we forgot."

When Bob left later that afternoon, Rachel thanked him for helping her with her homework.

"No problem," he replied. "After all, I *am* a teacher. Don't hesitate to call if you need me."

This time that little grin wasn't so annoying.

"You know, Mom," said Rachel, closing the door, "I kind of like Bob. He's a nice guy."

Her mother brushed a wisp of hair from Rachel's face.

"I already knew that," she said.

From then on it didn't bother Rachel that Bob was around so much. He took her to the beach, the movies, and the county fair. He even went with her to an open house at school. It felt good to introduce her teacher to Bob and be able to say he was a teacher too. And when Rachel told Bob about Danny, the mean kid in class who sat behind her and pulled her ponytail, Bob taught her how to stand up for herself. Danny left her alone after that.

One Saturday Rachel and Tori were at the mall with Andrea again, eating French fries and going in and out of stores.

"Guess what," said Rachel.

"Huh?" Tori mumbled.

"My mom got engaged. She and Bob are getting married!"

"Really?" asked Tori. "Are you OK with that?"

"There was a time when I would have said no, but not anymore," said Rachel. "Like I always say, no one could ever take the place of my real dad, but I like Bob. He helps me with my homework and takes me places and stuff."

"Then he's the answer to your prayer," said Tori.

"Huh?" asked Rachel.

"Your prayer! You know, the one about finding another dad, and I told you it would never happen, and . . ."

Rachel felt a chill go up her spine.

"That's right!" she said. She turned toward the balcony and put both hands on the railing.

"I can't believe I didn't realize it until now," said Rachel. "Bob *is* the answer to my prayer! I just never made the connection. I was always asking for someone who was just like my dad, and Bob is totally different. He doesn't like to go camping, but I can talk to him about anything and he listens. He's also smart and funny and . . . I don't know . . . he's just really nice."

That afternoon when Rachel got home, she went into her room and closed the door. Then she knelt by her bed and gave thanks to the Lord. She knew she'd never forget that moment for the rest of her life. Her heart was filled with joy!

On the day of the wedding, Rachel got to stand next to her mother as maid of honor. She caught the bouquet, too, even though she knew the older girls let her have it on purpose. As she touched the tiny petals, they seemed to symbolize everything good in her life. They were a symbol of love, family, and answered prayer.

Jesus really was listening to me all along, Rachel thought to herself. *I should have known he'd answer if I didn't give up!*

The Parable of the Persistent Widow

LUKE 18:1-8

As you read in our story, Rachel really wanted to have a new dad after the death of her real father. She prayed night after night for a new daddy—but the Lord didn't seem to be listening. Prayer is sometimes like that. We want God to answer us in a hurry, but he sometimes takes more time.

What should we do when the Lord doesn't answer very quickly? The Bible tells us not to give up hope. We should keep on believing and praying. All of our prayers are being heard. The Lord is always listening, and he will do what is best when the time is right.

Jesus told us about faith in a story called "The Parable of the Persistent Widow." A persistent person is someone who never gives up—someone who just keeps coming back. The woman in this story had a problem that she wanted a judge to solve for her. She kept asking him about this problem, just like when you keep asking your mother and dad for something you want them to do. This woman bugged the judge day after day for an answer. Finally the judge got so tired of the woman bothering him that he did what she wanted.

This is the meaning of the parable. If a selfish judge would help someone just to get rid of the person, how much more God will help his own children, whom he loves. The Lord wants us to keep talking to him about the things that worry us because he cares about us very much. God never gets tired of hearing from us.

That's what Rachel learned when she prayed for a father. Her request was being answered even though she didn't understand what God had been doing. He was listening to her all the time!

Even when he doesn't do what we expect, God is listening and doing what is best.

What are you praying about?

JCD

The Wood-Carver's Visitor

Based on the Parable of the Good Samaritan

LUKE 10:30-37

long time ago on a mountain, high above a village, there lived a wood-carver and his son. The wood-carver's name was Eli, and he was very talented. He could make clocks, sculptures, and furniture with the simplest of tools.

Eight-year-old Jesse liked to help his father after school. He chopped wood, cleaned the shed, and took care of their dog, Old Blue. Eli often told Jesse how nice it was to have a son like him.

Every Saturday Eli and Jesse loaded their truck and drove to the village. Merchants paid top dollar for Eli's woodwork because he was the finest craftsman they had ever seen. Everyone respected him even though no one knew him very well. He was somewhat mysterious—a quiet man who chose to live in the mountains, away from people. He seemed a little strange, but most of the people in town admired his beautiful work.

One afternoon while Jesse was helping his father stack wood, a stranger strolled into the yard. "Hello," he said quietly.

Eli looked up from his work and wiped the sweat from his forehead. A thin man who was unshaved and poorly dressed stood in front of him. "Well, hello," Eli replied. "Can I help you?"

"I was wondering if I could trouble you for some water," said the stranger. "I don't know where to find a stream in these hills."

"Of course," said Eli. "Follow me." He led the man inside the cabin and gave him a drink.

"What brings you all the way up here?" Eli asked.

The stranger looked uncomfortable. "I'm traveling to visit my family," he said nervously. "Been walking for days. Still have many more miles to go."

"Sounds like you're on quite a journey," Eli remarked. "By the way, my name's Eli, and the boy outside is my son, Jesse. We'd be happy if you joined us for supper."

The man appeared relieved. "Thank you very much," he said as he glanced around the room. "Nice place you have here," he commented. "Lots of fine furniture."

"Thanks," said Eli. "I made those pieces myself."

The stranger's eyes widened. "Really?" he asked. "You could make a lot of money doing this."

Eli laughed. "It's a living," he said. "Been doing it so long I can hardly remember when I started. Perhaps you'd like to see my woodshed. I'm taking some things to town tomorrow to sell."

The man nodded and followed his new friend outside.

When Eli unlatched the shed door, the stranger stared in amazement. Lined up against the wall were the most beautiful pieces of furniture he'd ever seen. A china cabinet, dining table, some fancy chairs—each one perfectly carved. But what really caught his eye was the clock that hung on the wall.

The maple-wood sculpture, with its detailed design, looked as if it had required hours of carving and sanding. And the sound of the Westminster chimes added a majestic quality to it.

"That's a real beauty," said the stranger, pointing to the clock. "Are you going to sell that, too?"

Eli looked toward the wall and smiled. "No, I'll never sell that," he replied.

"I like to keep it in the shed because I spend so much time here. You see, that clock is very special to me. I made it for my wife the year she died. It was the last gift I ever gave her. . . ."

Eli walked to the clock and touched the smooth surface, almost as if he were touching his wife.

The stranger stood in silence, keeping his eyes fixed on the wooden master-piece.

After a few seconds Eli turned away from his creation. "So . . . are you ready to eat?" he asked.

"Uh, sure," the man answered. He took one last look at the clock as he followed Eli back to the house.

Jesse helped his father prepare the evening meal, and they sat down for supper.

After Eli prayed a blessing, the stranger stabbed a bite with his fork and popped it into his mouth. The food had a unique, salty flavor.

"What kind of meat is this?" he asked.

"It's venison," answered Eli.

"What's that?" asked the man.

"Deer meat!" laughed Jesse.

The stranger looked embarrassed as he lowered his eyes toward his plate.

"Perhaps you'd like to take some with you on your journey," Eli suggested.

"I would," said the stranger. "Thank you."

After supper Eli prepared a basket of venison, bread, and cheese for the man. He also gave him enough water to last a few days.

"You're welcome to stay here tonight if you'd rather leave in the morning," said Eli.

"Thanks, but I really need to go," said the man. He took the basket and turned to leave. On the way out, he passed their sleeping hound-dog on the porch.

"What's your dog's name?" asked the man.

"Old Blue," said Eli. "A good name for a bluetick hound, wouldn't you say?"

"Is he a good watchdog?" asked the stranger.

"Not anymore," said Eli. "He's up in years now, so we don't expect much out of him—just his loyalty." Eli chuckled as he bent down to give his dog a pat.

"I'll be on my way now," said the stranger. "Thanks again for everything."

"You're welcome," said Eli. "And good luck!" He and Jesse waved good-bye as the man disappeared into the setting sun.

Much later that night, Eli awoke to the sound of Old Blue scratching at the front door. Then a loud crash came from the woodshed.

"What is it, Papa?" asked Jesse, switching on the light.

"I don't know," said his father. "Stay here!" He grabbed his shotgun and went outside to investigate.

Old Blue headed straight for the woodshed and began to bark.

As Eli squinted his eyes, he could see the shadow of a man running through the darkness.

"A thief," he whispered.

He hurried to the shed and turned on the light. Sure enough, someone had been there—the Westminster clock was gone. And Eli knew who had stolen it!

Jesse was barefoot on the porch when his father returned to the house. "What was it, Papa?" he asked. "What happened?"

Eli shook his head and sighed. "Our guest turned out to be a thief," he said sadly. "The clock has been stolen."

He glanced at Old Blue, who was looking up at his master and panting heavily. "Good job, boy," said Eli, scratching him behind the ears. "At least nothing *else* was stolen. You're a better watchdog than I thought."

Blue seemed to understand the compliment, drumming his tail against the door.

■   ■   ■

Somewhere down the mountain the stranger was escaping with his prize. Under his arm was the wood-carver's clock. He held it tightly as he hurried toward the village, trying to see through the black night.

Suddenly, a broken tree branch caused him to stumble! He fell forward and hit the ground hard, smashing the clock to pieces.

The man winced in pain as he pulled his twisted foot out from under the branch. "My ankle," he moaned. "It must be broken."

Through the darkness he could see a deep gash on the side of his leg. The blood trickled down his leg as his ankle began to swell. He stood up and tried to walk, but the injury brought him to the ground in pain. He tried again with the same result. Exhaustion was beginning to over-take him.

Anxiously he looked around for help. In the distance, a tiny light was flickering through the trees.

Maybe someone lives there, he said to himself. He began to crawl on his hands and knees in the direction of the light. As he got closer, he could see it was coming from a cabin near the main road. After much effort, the stranger managed to get to the front porch. He hugged a post tightly and slowly pulled himself to his feet. Taking a deep breath, he used the last of his energy to knock on the door.

"Who is it?" a man's voice called out.

"I need help," said the stranger. "I've broken my ankle."

The door swung open to reveal a short, stocky man in striped pajamas. "Do you know what time it is?" he asked. "It's two o'clock in the morning!"

"Yes," said the stranger. "But I've been hurt—I need help."

The owner of the house saw the stranger standing on one foot, his leg bleeding.

"I'm sorry," he said flatly. "There isn't a thing I can do for you at this time of night. Besides, how do I know I can trust you? I'm afraid I'm going to have to ask you to leave."

Before the man shut the door, the stranger noticed a plaque on the wall. It said, "To Mayor George Fenmor for four years of dedicated service."

The mayor of the village, the stranger thought. *I knew I'd seen that face. He certainly didn't give* me *any dedicated service.*

He glanced at his ankle. It had now swelled to three times its normal size. *Maybe if I wait by the road, somebody will help me,* he reasoned.

He made it to the roadside and collapsed. His ankle was throbbing, and his body began to shiver in the cold night air. By the time the sun came up, he was barely conscious.

Several cars passed by, but no one stopped to see why a man was lying by the roadside.

Finally a truck driver slowed down to investigate. Seeing that the man was injured, the driver lifted him from the ground and carried him to the truck. He placed the stranger in the passenger's seat and then got a blanket and wrapped it around the man's body for warmth.

Through bleary eyes the stranger looked into his rescuer's face—it was Eli! And standing next to him was Jesse.

The stranger tried to speak. "You . . . I thought . . ."

"Shh," said Eli. "Don't try to talk. We're going to take you to a doctor."

"You'll be OK, mister," added Jesse. "My dad will get you there in no time."

Eli drove to the village and located the office of the town physician. The doctor helped carry the man inside and examined his leg.

"We'll take care of him right away," said the doctor. "The ankle is broken, and I'll need to stitch up the gash on the leg."

"OK," said Eli. "I'll come back tomorrow to check on his condition. And make sure I get the bill; I'll see that it's paid."

When Eli returned the following day, the stranger was sitting in bed with his ankle in a cast. A device was attached to keep it elevated.

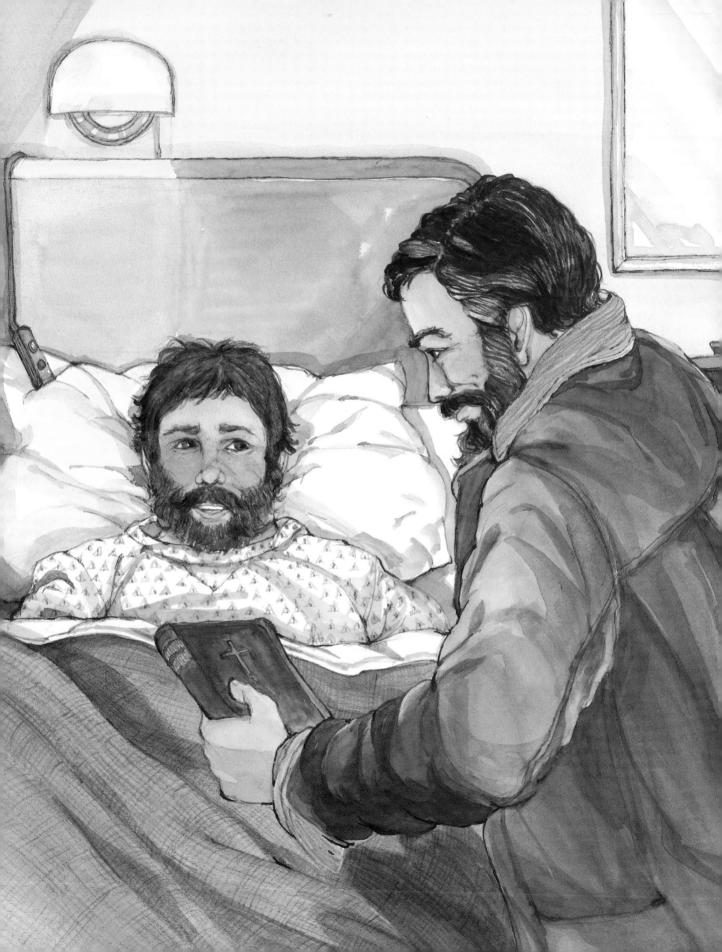

Eli smiled and sat down in a nearby chair. In his hand was a leather-bound Bible. "How are you feeling today?" he asked.

The stranger cleared his throat. "Much better," he answered. "Where's Jesse?"

"His Sunday school class went on a picnic," said Eli. "I'll bring him by later."

The man nodded. Then his expression grew very serious, as if he suddenly remembered something important. He looked at Eli with questioning eyes.

"Why?" he asked. "Why did you help me after I stole something that meant so much to you?"

Eli paused before answering. He looked down at the Bible and back up again.

"It's not easy for me to care for someone I don't know," he said. "Especially when that person has stolen something precious to me. But Jesus told us to love God with all of our heart and to love our neighbor as ourselves. That is why I have cared for you despite what you did."

"But I don't know how to repay you," said the stranger. "I can't even give you your clock back—it broke when I fell."

"You needn't repay me," Eli said. "There is one thing you can do, though. You can tell me your name."

The stranger smiled. "My name is Ray. Ray Parker."

Eli shook his hand. "Do you live around here?" he asked.

"Yes," answered Ray. "My family and I live on the other side of the village, just a few miles from here."

"Then you're a local," said Eli. "Good! Perhaps we can get to know each other better."

Ray's eyes seemed to brighten. "I'd like that," he said.

Eli lifted the Bible from his lap and placed it on the bed table. "This is a gift for you," he said. "I hope you'll find time to read it."

Ray lifted the book from the table and flipped through the pages. "Yes, I sure will," he said.

As the months went by, news about what Eli had done for Ray traveled throughout the village. People no longer thought of the wood-carver as a mysterious, quiet man who stayed away from people. They began using words like *thoughtful, caring,* and *good neighbor* to describe him.

No one understood Eli better than Ray Parker. He had seen with his own eyes the actions of a caring neighbor and the true meaning of Christian love.

The Parable of the Good Samaritan

LUKE 10:30-37

This story about Eli and his son, Jesse, is very important. It is based on Jesus' parable about a Jewish man who was traveling on a country road one day. Suddenly a band of robbers jumped on him and beat him badly. They took his clothes and left him lying half dead by the side of the road.

Pretty soon a priest came by the hurt man. He just went on his way, acting as if he didn't notice. Another religious man came by in a few hours and also passed by the bloody traveler. These two men left the wounded man to die.

But then a third man came by. He was from the country of Samaria. Jewish people hated the Samaritans, just like some people today hate those who are different from them. The Samaritan had every reason not to help the hurt traveler, but he bandaged the man's wounds and took him to get food and medicine. Jesus was pleased by the love and care given by the Samaritan.

In Danae's story Eli and his son, Jesse, are like the man from Samaria. They showed love to someone who was hard to love. The man had stolen from them and had broken the clock that Eli's wife had cherished. Eli could have left the stranger lying by the road after the accident, but he and his son did what Jesus wanted them to do. They took the man to a doctor and showed kindness to him. And because of their love, they were able to teach him about Jesus and the Bible.

What will you do if you run into someone who has been unkind to you? When that happens, remember the story of the Good Samaritan. He helped the wounded stranger even though the people from that man's country hated the Samaritans. That is exactly what Jesus would want you to do.

JCD

The Angry Sister

Based on the Parable of the Unforgiving Servant

MATTHEW 18:23-35

The sound of pounding feet echoed throughout the house.

Six-year-old Ashley leaped across the room and tagged her little sister on the back. "You're it!" she shouted.

Chelsea, who was two years younger, spun around and began chasing her sister in the opposite direction. The two girls slid across the hardwood floors, squealing and laughing.

Their mother was talking on the phone when they came flying through the kitchen. She took the receiver away from her ear for a moment. "Calm down, girls! You're going to break something," she warned.

"Don't worry," said Ashley. "We won't break anything." She clutched the door as her legs swung into the next room.

Chelsea wasn't fast enough to catch her big sister, so she stopped running and hid behind a bookcase. When Ashley walked by a few minutes later, Chelsea jumped out and grabbed her around the knees.

"Tag!" she yelled. "You're it!"

She stood and began to giggle and run the other way.

Ashley couldn't believe she'd been outsmarted! She took off after Chelsea as fast as she could, stretching her arm to try to make contact. Suddenly she tripped over a footstool and fell against her sister. The two girls plunged to the floor, knocking down and breaking a crystal lamp.

Chelsea immediately began to cry. When Mother came into the room, she found both girls sprawled on the floor, surrounded by glass.

"What have you done?" she exclaimed.

After making sure there were no cuts or broken bones, their mother leaned down and began picking up pieces of the lamp. "This belonged to my grandma," she said. "Do you realize you broke an expensive antique? It was priceless!"

Ashley had big tears in her eyes. "I did it, Mommy," she said. "But I didn't mean to."

"You were disobedient," said her mother. "I told you to calm down, and you wouldn't listen. Now you've destroyed something valuable. You're just lucky you didn't hurt yourself or your sister."

Ashley looked at Chelsea, who was still breathing hard. Her face was red and soaking wet with tears.

Mother pointed toward the back of the house. "Ashley, I want you to stay in your room until your dad gets home," she said. "And, Chelsea, go sit in the corner until I tell you to get up."

Ashley walked away, keeping her head down in shame. When she reached her bedroom, she noticed Miss Molly in the wicker chair. Miss Molly was Ashley's favorite doll, made of fine porcelain. Pretty blonde curls surrounded her delicate face, and the dress she wore was long and frilly.

Mother had given the doll to Ashley for her birthday last year. Miss Molly was not a toy to be played with—she was breakable. That's why Mother told her to always be careful.

Ashley sat down in the wicker chair and placed the doll on her lap.

"I was naughty today," she said, winding one of Miss Molly's curls around her finger. "I didn't obey my mother, and then I broke her lamp. I hope she isn't too angry with me."

Ashley mumbled a few more words before falling asleep in the chair. She woke up when her father opened the door. He sat down on the bed, still wearing the suit and tie he had worn at the office.

"Your mother told me what happened," he said.

Ashley sat up in the chair and squeezed her doll tight. "I'm sorry, Daddy," she said. "You can take all the money in my piggy bank—and my allowance, too."

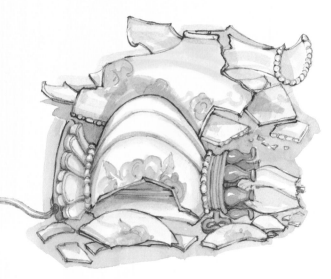

Her father shook his head. "I don't think three dollars a week is going to pay for the lamp," he said. "At least not for a long time. But there's a bigger issue here. You were disobedient."

Ashley bit her lip and looked down at the floor. She felt her father's finger under her chin, tilting her head up. He had a slight smile on his face.

"I think you've learned your lesson this time," he said.

Just then, Mother and Chelsea came into the room. Ashley looked at her mom and began to cry. "I'm sorry," she said.

"I know you are," said her mother. "I forgive you."

"Y-you're not going to punish me?" asked Ashley.

"No," answered her mother, smiling. "I don't think you meant to do wrong."

Ashley got up and hugged her parents. "I love you, Mommy! And I love you, too, Daddy!" she said.

Chelsea looked as if she was feeling left out, so Ashley gave her a hug too. It sure felt good to be forgiven and accepted again.

During the next few weeks, Ashley tried to play games with her sister that weren't so rowdy. They had fun with Tinkertoys, Barbie dolls, and tea parties. Everything was running smoothly in the family. Until one day . . .

■ ■ ■

Ashley was coming down the hallway when she heard a noise in her room. It sounded like someone singing! The door was almost closed, except for a crack where a sliver of light was shining into the hall. Ashley put her hand on the knob and slowly pushed it open. There stood Chelsea in the middle of the room, with her back to the door. She was singing a lullaby.

Rock-a-bye, baby, in the treetop,
When the wind blows, the cradle will rock. . . .

She seemed to have something in her arms as she swayed back and forth. When Ashley got closer, she gasped! Chelsea was holding Miss Molly!

"Chelsea!" her sister shouted. "That's *my* doll! Give her to me!"

A startled Chelsea jumped with fear. Her arms flew out, causing Miss Molly to fall to the floor. A piece of porcelain chipped off the doll's face!

"Look what you did!" cried Ashley, scooping up her favorite possession. She pressed Miss Molly to her chest and began to sob.

Chelsea looked frightened. Her mouth was open, and all the color was gone from her face. "I'm sorry," she said timidly.

"Get out!" said Ashley. "Just go away!" She buried her face in the doll's curls and cried and cried.

Mother heard the commotion and hurried into the bedroom.

Ashley held up her doll. "Look what Chelsea did! She *broke* it!"

Mother surveyed the damage. "Oh, I'm sorry," she said. "What happened?"

Ashley explained the story through short breaths, trying to choke back the tears. "Chelsea isn't supposed to be in my room," she sniffed. "Not unless I say so."

Mother turned to her younger daughter. "That's true, Chelsea," she said. "Why were you in Ashley's room without asking?"

The little girl didn't say anything. She just stood there, twisting her fingers in her other hand.

Ashley glared at her sister. "You broke Miss Molly, and you're going to pay for it," she snapped. "I want all the money in your piggy bank!"

Chelsea made a face as if she were going to cry. "I don't have any," she said.

"Then I want your allowance every week so I can buy a new doll!" said Ashley.

"Just a minute," said Mother, interrupting. "We can discuss this at dinner tonight. For now, I think the two of you should spend some time apart from each other. And don't cry about the doll, Ashley. We'll work something out."

But Ashley did cry about the doll—all afternoon as a matter of fact. When she wasn't crying, she was pouting or moping around the house. By the time supper rolled around, her mood was even worse. She sat hunched over in the chair, pushing peas around her plate with her fork.

"Please stop playing with your food," said her father.

Ashley laid her silverware down and crossed her arms. "I'm not hungry right now," she announced.

"Your sister didn't mean to break your doll," said her father. "It was an accident."

"But she wasn't supposed to be in my room," said Ashley. "And she wasn't supposed to play with my things—especially Miss Molly!"

"Chelsea apologized," said Mother. "I think it's time to forgive and forget."

"No! No! No!" said Ashley. "I won't forgive her. Ever! Not unless she pays for my doll with her allowance."

"OK," said Mother. "That's fair. But I've been meaning to tell you that I want *your* allowance too."

Ashley looked confused. "Why?" she asked.

"Wasn't it just a few weeks ago that you broke my crystal lamp?" asked her mother. "It was much more expensive than your doll. Did I refuse to forgive you until you replaced it? Did I demand that you give me your allowance money?"

Ashley realized she no longer had an argument. She sat in silence for a long time, just staring at her plate. Finally she looked at Chelsea and sighed.

"OK," she said. "I forgive you. And you don't have to pay for breaking my doll."

The corners of Chelsea's mouth turned upward in a huge grin. She got up from her chair and hugged her sister around the neck.

"I'm really sorry about Miss Molly," she whispered.

"We'll take her to a repair shop tomorrow," said Mother. "They can fix the damage so she'll be as good as new."

Ashley squealed with delight. "Thanks, Mommy!" she said.

She took her sister by the hand. "Come on, let's go play!"

"Wait a minute," said her dad. "You need to finish your dinner first."

Ashley made a face. "OK," she said. "But do I have to eat the peas?"

Her father smiled and let out a deep breath. "Not tonight," he said.

The Parable of the Unforgiving Servant

MATTHEW 18:23-35

When someone has hurt you badly or made you very angry, what do you feel like doing? I can guess. You want to hurt that person back, don't you? Something inside makes you want to get even. But that isn't what the Bible tells us to do. The Lord wants us to forgive others because he has forgiven our many sins.

Jesus told a parable that will help you understand his forgiveness. It is a story about a servant who owed a great amount of money to a powerful king. When the servant couldn't pay, the king ordered this man and his entire family to be sold into slavery. The man had a big problem!

The servant fell on his knees and begged the king to be understanding. "Please, please, sir," he said. "Give me some time to pay back what I owe."

The king took pity on the man and forgave his entire debt. But as the servant was leaving the palace, he saw another man who owed him just a little amount of money. Instead of being kind the way the king had been to him, the servant threw this other man into prison until he could pay.

Because the servant had showed no kindness after he had been forgiven so much, the king became very angry. He threw the wicked servant in prison until he was able to pay every cent of his debt.

Jesus told this parable to explain how strongly God feels about forgiveness. Unless we are willing to forgive others, God will not forgive the sin in our lives.

Now you can understand how wrong it was for Ashley to stay angry at her sister for breaking her china doll. Ashley's mother had forgiven her for smashing the lamp, but Ashley did not want to forgive Chelsea for what she had done.

Remember this: If we will not forgive others, then God will not forgive us. This is what Jesus teaches us in the parable of the unforgiving servant.

JCD

The
Talent Search

Based on the Parable of the Talents

MATTHEW 25:14-30

**T**he afternoon sun glistened through the windows of the fourth-grade Sunday school room.

Deann Lee sat in the back row, half paying attention as her teacher read the announcements. It wasn't that Deann didn't like Mrs. Kessler; it was just that it was almost time to leave and Deann was hungry for lunch. She tapped her foot silently on the carpet, a habit she had when she felt anxious.

As she glanced down at her Bible, she suddenly heard two words that caused her to look up again: *talent show!*

Mrs. Kessler explained that the children's department needed money for summer Bible camp. Not all the children could afford to go, so the department staff was organizing a talent show as a fund-raiser. It would take place next month, and everyone in the class could participate.

Deann's heart began to beat faster. *A talent show!* she thought. *What a great idea!*

Until now, Deann had given up her desire to go to camp. With three younger brothers, there wasn't a lot of extra money for activities like that.

She began to envision herself at the talent show, hearing the roar of applause while spotlights shone on her face. She saw herself smiling and leaning forward to take a bow or—better yet—a curtsy.

Deann smiled at the thought, but it wasn't long before her fantasy evaporated like a puff of smoke. She suddenly realized there was no way she could be in the show. For one thing, Deann didn't have a talent. She couldn't sing, couldn't act, couldn't dance, and couldn't play an instrument. And if that wasn't bad enough, there was another problem to consider—sometimes when Deann felt nervous, she stuttered.

Mrs. Kessler reminded everyone that the first rehearsal would be held one week from Saturday. Then she said a short prayer and dismissed the class.

As Deann started to leave, her friends Tiffany and Rochelle met her at the door.

"Won't this be fun?" said Tiffany. "I've been taking gymnastics for five years now. We do a lot of routines for charity, so I can use one for the talent show."

"I think I'm going to do a violin solo," said Rochelle. "I already played it in a church recital this year."

Both girls turned their attention to Deann. "What about you, Dee?" asked Rochelle. "What are you going to do?"

Deann gave her best smile and tried to act confident. "I-I don't really know yet," she replied. "I haven't d-decided on anything."

"You don't have much time," Tiffany warned. "Rehearsals start less than two weeks from now."

"I know," said Deann. "I heard what Mrs. K-Kessler said."

Tiffany and Rochelle got lost in their conversation and walked ahead of Deann, discussing ideas for music and costumes. They were so excited that they were both talking at the same time!

Deann headed to the parking lot. When she got there, she saw her family in the van with the engine running.

One of her brothers leaned out the sliding door. "Hurry up, slowpoke!" he commanded. "We're hungry!"

Deann climbed into the van and plopped down on a velvety seat.

"Hi, honey," said her mother. "How was Sunday school?"

"It was OK," answered Deann.

"What sounds good for lunch today, kids?" asked her father.

The younger children voted for McDonald's.

As the Aerostar van pulled up to the drive-through lane, everyone began giving their orders at once. "One at a time, please," said Mr. Lee.

It turned out that everyone wanted the same thing— a Happy Meal with McNuggets and a vanilla shake.

But Deann ordered only fries because her stomach felt a little queasy. To make matters worse, two of her brothers got into a fight over who got the best Happy Meal toy. They began to argue and shove each other in the backseat.

Mrs. Lee turned around so she could see them. "That's enough, boys," she said. "You will sit and eat quietly, do you understand?"

"Yes, Mom," they said in unison.

"Speaking of quiet, you've hardly said two words, Deann. Are you sure you're all right?" Her mother looked concerned.

Deann sighed. "I'm just not very hungry," she replied. "I'll eat something later."

Deann turned her face to the window and watched the trees whiz by.

What am I going to do? she thought to herself. *All the kids in my Sunday school class are going to be in the talent show except me. I have to think of something!*

Mr. Lee pulled the van into the concrete driveway and turned off the engine. The younger children jumped out and began running toward the house. Deann lingered behind to pick up the trash and half-eaten McNuggets that were lying on the seats. Since she was the oldest, there were certain jobs she accepted as her duty.

She threw the trash away and headed upstairs to her bedroom, tripping over a dirty sneaker on the way.

"Why don't I have any talent, God?" she asked, closing the door behind her. "Isn't there *one* thing I'm good at?"

Deann plopped down in a chair and sighed, picking at a piece of thread on her dress. "Why does life have to be so complicated?" she said out loud.

The following Sunday, Deann's class was all abuzz about the talent show. The first rehearsal was only six days away. After church Deann walked over to the sign-up sheet that was posted on the bulletin board. There were lots of signatures scribbled in blue, purple, green, and black ink. Deann wished she could write her own name on the paper, but what would she volunteer to do? Clean up?

Just then she felt a hand on her shoulder. She turned to see Mrs. Kessler smiling at her.

"Are you going to be in the talent show?" she asked.

"No," answered Deann sadly.

Her Sunday school teacher pointed to the sign-up sheet. "Why don't you sign up to be master of ceremonies?" she asked.

"What's that?" asked Deann.

"It's an important part in the show," said Mrs. Kessler. "The emcee gets to stay on stage the entire time, introducing the other kids and making all the announcements. You have a fun personality, and you read very well. I think you'd be good at it."

Deann bit her lip. "I-I don't know," she replied. "It sounds like an awfully b-big job."

"Well, think about it and let me know," said Mrs. Kessler. Then she turned to speak to a parent.

Deann looked at the sign-up sheet again. *Master of ceremonies,* she said to herself. *I'd have to stay on stage the whole time. . . . No! I couldn't do it—what if I got nervous and stuttered? I'd get laughed off the stage!*

Rochelle walked over and tapped her on the shoulder. "Hi, Dee," she said. "Have you decided what you're going to do for the show?"

Before she could answer, Tiffany waltzed over and stood beside them. She had a big smile on her face. Deann wished she could take a cloth and wipe it right off!

"What did you sign up for, Dee?" she asked.

Deann swallowed hard and locked her jaw. "I'm not going to be in it," she said boldly. "I've got too much homework this week."

"We've got homework too, Dee," said Rochelle. "Is there some other reason?"

Deann pretended she didn't hear her friend as she looked at her Minnie Mouse watch. "I have to go," she said. "Last week I was late and . . . well, you know how impatient my little brothers can be."

"Well, OK," said Rochelle. "But you're going to miss a lot of fun at the talent show. We're going to have ice cream at Mrs. Kessler's house afterwards."

Deann said good-bye and hurried toward the parking lot. She thought about how she hadn't stuttered once in front of Tiffany and Rochelle. Deep down inside, Deann wanted to be a part of the talent show more than anything. The thought of being the emcee was much too scary, though. It was a risk she wasn't willing to take.

The following Saturday, Deann was eating cereal and watching cartoons with her brothers. Her father came into the kitchen to pour a cup of coffee.

"I'm going to church for a meeting this afternoon," he said. "I have to leave right after lunch."

All of a sudden, Deann had an idea! Why not go and watch the kids rehearse for the talent show? It might be fun to see the excitement even if she wasn't participating.

Later Deann put on one of her favorite outfits and hitched a ride to the church with her dad. When she got there, she entered Richmond Hall and took a seat in the back row. Someone named Marcy was singing "Amazing Grace." Deann didn't think the girl's voice was very good, but she admired her courage.

After that, there were a ballet dancer, a magician, and a trombone player. Then Tiffany and Rochelle got on stage and did their routines perfectly! Deann was surprised that she didn't feel a little bit jealous. She was really proud of her friends.

Finally, Mrs. Kessler announced the final category—master of ceremonies.

Deann watched the contestants very closely. The first person was a little shy, and the second was a bit too dramatic.

I could do a better job than that, Deann said to herself. *Maybe there's still time for me to try out.*

Then a frightening thought came to her mind. It was so scary it made her heart skip a beat. *What if I fail?* she thought. *I might stutter or maybe even trip on the stage!*

Deann began to tap her foot. There was no carpet on the cement floor, so it made an annoying sound. She was thinking too hard to notice, though. Deann knew she had to make a fast decision.

She bowed her head and closed her eyes. "Dear God," she whispered, "I'd really like to be in the show. I know I don't have much talent, but I'd still like to give it a try. Please help me to do a good job. Amen."

When Deann finished praying, she stood up and began politely inching her way past knees and feet. She hurried backstage to the changing room and bolted through the door. Mrs. Kessler was helping one of the girls out of her costume. When she heard Deann come in, she stopped and turned around.

"Deann!" she exclaimed. "I didn't expect to see you here!"

The young girl put her hand on her chest and took a deep breath. "Mrs. Kessler, I'm not on the list, but I *know* I could do a good job as master of ceremonies! Can I try out for the part? *Please?*"

Mrs. Kessler smiled and picked up a copy of the script. Then she handed it to Deann and said, "Of course you can. You have about five minutes to look it over."

Deann forgot all about her fear as she waited for her big moment.

The last one to try out, she walked to the center of the stage and flashed a big, toothy smile at the Sunday school staff.

When Deann read from the script, her words were clear, and her voice was strong and confident. She didn't stutter or make one mistake! As she left the stage, Deann was thankful to God for her performance. She had discovered a gift, a talent he had given her that she could call her own.

Nobody was surprised when the news came that Deann had been chosen master of ceremonies. During the next couple weeks, Deann rehearsed her part along with the others. She said each person's name very clearly and practiced hard on all of the announcements. On the night of the talent show, she recited all her lines *from memory* and did a great job! It was hard to believe there was a time when she didn't think she could do it!

Everyone came out to take a bow after the performance. Deann was last because she had the biggest role in the show. As spotlights shone on her face, she gracefully bowed *and* curtsied. She saw her family in the second row. Out of the corner of her eye she could also see Mrs. Kessler, Tiffany, and Rochelle behind the curtain. They were all clapping. It was just like Deann had hoped it would be. The only difference was that now she didn't care about being the most important person in the show. She was just happy she had found a talent and a good way to use it. The money raised by the talent show would help many kids—including herself and two of her brothers—to go to Bible camp.

Deann had discovered how good it felt to do something for her church and for the Lord. She couldn't wait for the next opportunity to use the special talent God had given her. But for now her mind was focused on only one thing—the ice cream that was waiting at Mrs. Kessler's house!

The Parable of the Talents

MATTHEW 25:14-30

Jesus' parable about the talents is a story about three servants. Their master gave them money to use while he was gone. He wanted them to earn more money with it. When he got back, he was very pleased to find that two of the servants had doubled the amount he had given them. But the third servant buried his money in the ground instead of earning more. The master was very angry with that servant. He punished him for being lazy, and he took away everything he had given the man.

Do you understand the meaning of this story? Jesus was not really talking about people who waste money. He was teaching us not to waste our talents. What are talents? They are "gifts" or skills that have been given to us for the Lord's work. People who are lazy or afraid do not please God. They are wasting their talent, just like the servant did when he put his money in the ground.

That almost happened to Deann, who didn't think she had a talent even though her teacher told her she did. At first Deann was afraid to try out for the talent show. But when she finally did her part, she was thankful that she could use her gift to help others and to please God.

Many grown-ups make the mistake that Deann almost made. They won't work in the church or try to tell anyone about Jesus. The Lord wants us to be like the two servants who pleased their master by using wisely what they had been given.

What talents does Jesus, your Master, want you to use?

JCD

Puppy Love

Based on the Parable of the Lost Sheep

MATTHEW 18:12-14; LUKE 15:3-7

**I**t was a day that began like all the others.

Christian Roberts got up and went into the bathroom to wash his face. Then he combed his hair and yawned sleepily as he squeezed the toothpaste onto his toothbrush. At that moment he heard a soft knock on the bathroom door.

"Come in!" he said.

His mother opened the door a crack and poked her head inside.

"Good morning," she said cheerfully. "There's a surprise for you downstairs!" Her smile gave the secret away.

Suddenly Christian knew it would *not* be a day like all the others. "The puppies are born!" he exclaimed. Flinging his toothbrush into the sink, he hurried to the kitchen. There he saw the most wonderful sight! His dog, Fritzi, was curled up on a blanket. By her side were five furry little creatures all trying to nurse at once.

Christian knelt beside the puppies and studied them closely. All of them were white, except for one with a large black spot around one eye, and a black tail. The puppies' pink noses wiggled as they climbed over one another. Some of them were whimpering as they searched for their mother's milk.

"Look," said Christian. "They're all blind!"

"Yes," answered his mother. "Their eyes will stay closed for about ten days. God planned it that way so they'll be protected from light until they're more developed."

Christian reached out to pet one of the dogs.

"Grrrr!" growled Fritzi.

"Be careful, honey," said Mrs. Roberts. "Mother dogs don't like any smell that interferes with the scent of the litter. In a couple of weeks the puppies will be old enough for you to touch them."

"OK," Christian sighed. "But I wish I didn't have to wait."

Time went by quickly, and before long the puppies were running all over the backyard. Christian spent hours playing with them and taking them for rides in his wagon. At night he read them doggie stories even though he knew they couldn't understand the words. Christian grew to love the puppies very much.

Each one was special and different from the others. Candy was a sweet puppy, who often licked Christian's hand. Elmo liked to lie on his back and be tickled. Spirit was the friskiest pup—always running in circles or playing with a chew toy. Then there was Snoozer, who enjoyed sleeping all day.

Christian had named the black-and-white puppy Oreo because of his markings. Unfortunately, Oreo was a naughty puppy! He barked too much and was constantly getting into mischief. He chewed up Christian's socks and nibbled on Mrs. Roberts's plants. The worst thing was that he was always trying to get outside! Anytime the front door was open, Oreo wandered into the yard. Christian tried to teach him to stay in the house or the backyard, but the little dog paid no attention. He enjoyed smelling the garden flowers and going wherever he pleased.

Christian and his mother tried to keep the front door closed, but sometimes they forgot. And Oreo always managed to sneak past them when they weren't watching.

"That naughty dog is going to end up learning a lesson the hard way," Mrs. Roberts would always remark.

One cloudy afternoon she returned from the store with two bags of groceries. Hurrying to the kitchen, she placed them on the counter and put her keys in her purse.

The door! she thought to herself.

By the time Christian's mother returned to the front entrance, it was too late—Oreo was gone! Mrs. Roberts searched all over the yard but couldn't find him anywhere.

Christian knew all of Oreo's favorite sniffing places, but the boy hadn't come home from school yet.

Anxiously, Mrs. Roberts looked around the neighborhood. She even walked down the street and called his name, but Oreo was nowhere to be found.

By the time Christian arrived home from school, the dog had been gone more than an hour. The boy knew something was wrong when he saw his mother on her hands and knees, peering under a bush.

"Did Oreo get out again?" he asked.

"Yes," answered his mother. "He's been gone a long time. I've looked every-where, but I don't know where he could be."

"We have to find him!" exclaimed Christian. "He could have been stolen or hit by a car!"

"I know," said Mother. "But it's going to rain soon, so get your jacket."

Christian hurried into the house. When he got there, Fritzi met him at the door with the other puppies. She looked restless and worried.

"It's OK, girl," said Christian. "I'll find your baby. I promise!"

■　■　■

Meanwhile, Oreo was trotting down a nearby street. He felt so free and happy! A hundred new smells greeted his nostrils. This was the most exciting day of his young life—to be able to explore the great outdoors and go wherever he wanted.

Every once in a while a raindrop fell on his nose, but Oreo hardly noticed. There were too many things to sniff and chew.

With every step, the little dog got farther away from home. Before long, big clouds rolled in from the north, and darkness fell across the sky.

Oreo stopped walking and looked behind him. He suddenly felt afraid as he real-ized he was lost! He glanced to the right and then to the left, but nothing looked familiar.

His mouth was dry, and he began to pant. He had no idea how to get back home.

Oh, how he longed for his mother!

Oreo became so frightened that he started to run as fast as he could—but in the wrong direction! He sped past houses and streetlamps as he raced down the side-walk. A huge dog snarled and growled from behind a fence, which made him run even faster.

Suddenly a loud crash of thunder echoed above his head. The rain began to pour down from the sky, making it difficult to see anything. Oreo continued splashing along the sidewalk, doing his best to keep going.

Soon he came to a construction site where some workers had been building houses. The little dog had no idea he was headed straight for a ditch! There were signs and yellow tape all around it to warn people to be careful, but Oreo couldn't read them.

As he made his way around the hole, the edge gave way, causing him to slip in the mud. In a matter of seconds the entire side caved in and carried the little dog to the bottom!

He was trapped!

He tried to pull himself out, but his paws were unable to grip the slippery mud. The seven-week-old puppy just wasn't strong enough to escape. Tired and scared, Oreo finally stopped struggling and curled up at the bottom of the ditch, shivering and wet.

■　■　■

Back at the house, Christian and his mother continued to search for the lost puppy. Mrs. Roberts made telephone calls to neighbors while Christian got his bicycle out of the garage. He rode up and down the wet street, shining his flash-light in all directions. But it was no use—Oreo was gone.

Finally Mrs. Roberts called her son in from the rain. "You're going to catch a cold out there," she warned. "I know you're concerned for Oreo, but you must take care of yourself."

"We can't leave the little puppy out there alone," Christian pleaded. "He's probably cold and scared and maybe even in danger."

"Let's hope not, honey," said his mother. "Someone may have found him and taken him in by now."

Mrs. Roberts saw the worried look in her son's eyes. Then she glanced at Fritzi, who was pacing back and forth by the door.

"Why don't we pray for Oreo?" Mrs. Roberts suggested. Mother and son held hands and asked God to protect their puppy.

"And please, God," Christian pleaded, "if Oreo is out there somewhere, help us to find him." Christian opened his eyes and looked up at his mother. She knew what he was thinking.

"All right," she sighed. "Let's get in the car and continue the search."

Up and down the neighborhood they drove, shining two flashlights into the darkness.

"Oreo! Here, Oreo!" Christian called.

There was no response.

It was almost eleven o'clock, and still there was no sign of the lost puppy.

"Let's drive to another street," said Mrs. Roberts. "Maybe Oreo tried to—"

"Wait!" Christian interrupted. "Look at that construction site! A puppy could get lost in lots of places around there. I want to go look!"

Mrs. Roberts turned off the car engine. "All right," she said. "Just for a few minutes."

Christian and his mother got out of the car and opened their umbrellas. They shined their flashlights in the direction of the site.

"Oreo! Here, boy!" Christian called.

Mother followed as the young boy started walking down the sidewalk, repeating the puppy's name. Suddenly he stopped and listened closely. In the distance he could hear a faint whimpering sound.

Could it be? he wondered. His boots splashed through the puddles as he began running in the direction of the noise. It seemed to be getting louder!

Christian turned to the right and then the left—where was it coming from?

Seeing the ditch, he ran over and peered inside—there was the little puppy, all muddy and shivering at the bottom of the hole.

"Oh, no!" Christian gasped.

With trembling hands he reached down and lifted the frightened dog into his arms. Christian didn't mind that mud was caked all over Oreo's fur. He pressed the quivering body against his chest and held him close.

"Poor little Oreo," he whispered. "Don't worry. You're going to be OK."

Christian zipped his raincoat over the puppy just as his mother caught up with him.

"Mom! I found Oreo! I found him!" he said.

A wet, furry head poked out of Christian's coat collar.

"Oh, I'm so glad!" said Mrs. Roberts.

They laughed and cried as they jogged back to the car together.

On the way home, Mrs. Roberts reached over and scratched Oreo's ears. "You're a naughty puppy, but I'm glad you're safe now," she said.

Christian gave Oreo a squeeze and patted him on the head.

At the house, Mrs. Roberts immediately washed and dried the little dog and bundled him in some blankets. Christian carried him to a heater so he could get warm.

The boy watched the other puppies playing nearby with their ball and squeaky toys. Then he looked at Oreo and breathed a sigh of relief. When he yawned, his mother pointed toward his bedroom. It had been a very long day.

Fritzi didn't notice. She just nuzzled her baby and licked his tiny face.

As Christian pulled the covers up to his chin, he knew he would be able to get a good night's sleep now. He was so glad his lost puppy was finally back home and safe in his care.

Little Oreo was happy too. He had learned that the outdoors can be a scary place—it was cold and dark out there! As he lay down to sleep, he snuggled up to his mother and closed his eyes. From now on he was going to try to be a good puppy . . . at least until he found another sock to chew!

The Parable of the Lost Sheep

MATTHEW 18:12-14; LUKE 15:3-7

Now that you've read Christian's story, let me ask you some questions. Why do you think he was so worried about his lost puppy? He had other dogs to play with. Why did Oreo matter so much to him? And why did Christian go out with his mother on a cold, rainy night looking for the little dog?

The reason is that Christian loved Oreo. He loved his other dogs too, but this one was in trouble. Christian wasn't going to stop searching for the puppy until he found him. It didn't matter that Oreo had been a naughty dog. Christian just knew that the scared, cold, hungry puppy needed help. I imagine you would have felt that way about your dog too.

Did you know that Jesus also cares about animals? He told a parable about a shepherd who carefully watched over a flock of 100 sheep. But one day a little lamb wandered away, just as Oreo did. The shepherd left the flock and began searching for the one that was lost. He found the lamb and brought him back to the safety of the flock.

Jesus' parable of the lost sheep has another message. He wants us to understand that each of God's children is important to him. As the shepherd cares for each little lamb, Jesus looks out for every one of us. He said in his parable that our Father in heaven does not want even one of us to be lost. He wants each of us to go to heaven.

Isn't it neat to know that Jesus is always looking out for you? Even when you feel scared and alone, like Oreo, Jesus your "shepherd" always knows what you need. You can count on him to be there for you!

JCD

Grandpa's Garden

Based on the Parable of the Sower

MATTHEW 13:3-8; MARK 4:3-8; LUKE 8:5-8

**T**he year was 1984. Summertime.

Dust clouds formed around the minivan as it traveled down a gravel road. Eight-year-old Lisa sat in the passenger's seat. In the distance she could see an older man waving enthusiastically. "There's Grandpa McClusky!" she exclaimed.

"Yes," said her mother, waving back. She parked the van and turned off the engine. "Run and give him a hug. I'll bring your things."

When Lisa reached her grandfather, she leaped into his arms! He picked her up and swung her around in a circle. "How's Grandpa's favorite girl?" he laughed. His big smile revealed a gold tooth glistening in the sun.

"I've missed you, Grandpa," said Lisa, squeezing his neck.

"I've missed you, too, sweetheart," he replied. "I'm so glad you're here!"

There was no one Lisa loved to visit more than Grandpa McClusky! He was the only person she knew who owned a farm—a *real* one with horses, pigs, and chickens. Something about being there gave her a special feeling. Maybe it was the smell of the fresh berries, or the feel of the wind in her hair, or the glow of the fireflies in the night. Or maybe it was just being with Grandpa. He always seemed to have a smile on his face and an exciting story to tell. Lisa looked forward to visiting him every summer.

Just then Mother appeared, carrying Lisa's jacket and suitcase.

"Hi, Dad," she said, kissing Lisa's grandfather on the cheek.

He placed his hands on both sides of her face. "You're looking as beautiful as ever, honey," he said. "It's so good to see you."

After a long chat and two cups of coffee, Mother said she had to be on her way. She was meeting Lisa's father at the airport for a business trip.

"Planes don't wait, you know," she said with a smile.

Lisa and her grandfather waved good-bye as Mother's minivan headed up the drive.

"Well," said Grandpa, ruffling the top of Lisa's hair, "what would you like to do first?"

Lisa didn't have to think about her answer. "Let's go horseback riding!" she exclaimed.

"I knew you'd say that," her grandfather laughed. "Come on! The horses are saddled and ready to go!"

All afternoon they rode through the Tennessee hills, stopping for lunch by a clear stream. Lisa listened while her grandfather told her stories and talked about God and the laws of nature. He sure had learned a lot in his 69 years!

Lisa looked up at the sky and felt a cool breeze blow through her hair. This was a day she wanted to remember forever, even though she was sore from four hours of riding!

That evening they had a barbecue under the stars while fireflies danced all around. Between bites of dinner Lisa told her grandfather about school, her friends, and even Bryan, the boy at church she had a crush on.

"You should play hard to get," said her grandfather, winking. "That's what your grandma did before we were married."

Lisa sat up in her chair. "Really?" she asked.

"Why, sure," said her grandfather. "But you're too young to worry about things like that now."

"I guess you're right," said Lisa, slumping back down in her chair again. "Do you miss Grandma?"

"I sure do, sweetheart," her grandfather answered. "It's hard to believe it's been three years since she went to heaven. She was a wonderful woman, and I'm so glad to know I'll be able to see her again someday."

"Me, too," said Lisa. "Because I miss her just like you do." She swallowed her last bite of food and wiped her mouth on a napkin.

Grandpa picked up her plate from the patio table. "Time to get some rest now," he said. "We've had a big day."

The next morning Lisa awoke to voices downstairs. She strained her ears to hear her grandfather giving Tom, the hired hand, his chores for the day. Quickly she got dressed and hurried to the kitchen. By then, Grandpa was fixing breakfast.

"Good morning, honey," he said, scrambling eggs in a skillet.

Lisa took a seat at the table. "Grandpa, I want to help," she said.

"What do you mean?" he asked.

"I heard you telling Tom what his chores were, and I thought there might be something for me to do too."

"Well," he said, chuckling, "there's *always* something to be done around here." He pulled up a chair and sat next to her. "How about helping me in the vegetable garden today?"

"OK," said Lisa. "As long as I don't have to weed—Mom makes me do that at home." She wrinkled her nose to show her displeasure.

"No weeding," said Grandfather. "Today we'll be picking ripe vegetables."

After breakfast Lisa carried two large baskets and followed her grandpa to the garden. It was filled with carrots, radishes, tomatoes, and corn. Everything was so colorful; it was obvious this garden had been given the best of care.

Lisa helped her grandfather pick the ripe produce and load the baskets. While they were working, something caught her eye—a withered tomato plant in a corner of the garden.

"Look, Grandpa," said Lisa, pointing.

The older man approached the plant and squatted down to investigate.

"Hmm," he said. "Looks like the soil is bad here." He picked up a handful of dirt and let it fall through his fingers. But Lisa saw that he couldn't dig down very far.

"What's the matter?" she asked.

"There are some rocks in this area," answered her grandfather. "Seeds don't thrive in rocky soil where they can't develop roots."

"Oh," said Lisa. "That makes sense."

Grandpa McClusky's expression changed, as though he was getting ready to say something important. "Did I ever tell you the story of the four sailors?" he asked.

"No," replied Lisa. "I don't think I've heard that one."

Her grandfather stood up and dusted the dirt off his hands. "Would you like to hear it?" he asked.

"Sure," said Lisa.

He took her by the hand and led her to a nearby log so that they could sit down.

Grandpa McClusky was quiet for a few moments. He took a deep breath and looked across the fields.

"A long time ago," he began, "from 1941 to 1945 our country was in a very bad war. It was known as World War II. Have you heard about it?"

Lisa nodded.

"Well," her grandfather continued, "during the war there were four men who joined the navy at the same time. Their names were Joe, William, George, and Charlie. These sailors served on the same ship, where they met and became friends. They were at sea for months at a time and helped win some battles that people still remember today. But it was a difficult period in their lives. Many men were killed, and the four men didn't know if they would live from one day to the next.

"At one of the darkest moments, their ship was struck by a torpedo. It blew a hole about five feet below the waterline. Fortunately, the four men escaped death because they were on the upper deck when the explosion occurred. But not everyone survived. The sailors mourned the loss of fellow seamen as they struggled to get the damaged ship back to harbor."

"That's a sad story," said Lisa.

"Yes," said her grandfather. "But God can use even terrible experiences for our good."

He cleared his throat and continued the story. "So, during this time of tragedy a chaplain came to bring hope and encouragement to the men who had survived. When the chaplain finished his message, he invited the sailors to stand if they wanted to learn how they could accept the Lord as their personal Savior.

"One by one the four sailors—Joe, William, George, and Charlie—stood to express an interest. In fact, many men got to their feet that day. It was a special moment, with a lot of emotion and a few tears. Afterward, they followed the chaplain into a small room so he could explain the gift of salvation.

"The war finally ended in 1945, and the men returned to their families. But with death and destruction no longer a threat, three of the four friends forgot about the significance of that day. William eventually became an alcoholic, Charlie married a woman who got him into a false religion, and George just lost interest."

"What about the fourth sailor?" asked Lisa.

Her grandfather had a mischievous look in his eyes. He folded his arms and leaned close to her. "You're looking at him!" he said.

Lisa's mouth opened wide. "You?" she asked. "You mean that's a true story?"

"Every word," answered her grandfather. "After all, my name is *Joe* McClusky."

"Yes, but . . . I guess I didn't think of that before," said Lisa. "Did your friends William, George, and Charlie ever change?"

"I'd like to think they did," said her grandfather. "I've lost touch with them, but I sure hope they've gotten their lives straightened out with Jesus. They'll never find real happiness until they do.

"You see, honey, some people hear the Word, but things in life lead them astray. Just like the seed that falls on bad soil. It won't grow among rocks, thorns, or dry ground where it can't take root. But if it lands on good soil, it will produce a crop up to 100 times the amount sown."

"Like you, Grandpa?" asked Lisa.

Her grandfather chuckled as he looked across the fields. "I've grown a few good crops in my day," he said. "But there's a deeper meaning that I hope you understand."

"I do," said Lisa. "Your friends really didn't want to follow Jesus, so the 'seed' in their hearts couldn't grow. But when the chaplain planted a 'seed' in *your* heart, it grew and grew—just like the vegetables in your garden. And now you've learned to love Jesus a lot."

"That's exactly right, Lisa," said her grandfather. "I'm proud of you. Now, would you like to have lunch with an old sailor?"

"Sure," said Lisa. "What are we having?"

"The same thing I ate at sea for three years—navy beans!" answered her grandfather.

Lisa looked at him with a puzzled expression.

Grandpa McClusky burst out laughing. "Just kidding," he said. "Would you settle for a hamburger instead?"

The Parable of the Sower

MATTHEW 13:3-8; MARK 4:3-8; LUKE 8:5-8

Isn't it sad that the three sailors in Grandpa's story never became Christians? The chaplain had explained to each man how he could accept Jesus Christ as his personal Savior, but they all went their own way. Only the fourth sailor, Lisa's grandfather, repented of his sins and became a believer. He began serving the Lord as a young man and continued for many, many years.

Unfortunately, many people are like the sailors who rejected God's forgiveness and salvation. They just don't care, or else they don't understand. This is what Jesus was explaining in his parable of the sower. He described a farmer, called a "sower," who spread seeds on the ground. Some of them didn't grow because they fell in rocky places. Other seeds were choked by thorns and thistles. But the farmer scattered some of the seeds on good soil, and they grew into healthy plants.

Jesus' parable of the sower is clear. Some people hear about God's great love, but they reject it. Their seed falls on rocky and thorny land and it dies. But other people accept the Word of the Lord. The seed takes root in their lives and continues to grow.

Lisa's grandfather was one of those people who had very good soil in his heart. What about yours?

JCD

It's a Party—
Will You Come?

Based on the Parable of the Wedding Banquet

MATTHEW 22:1-14

Kevin Sanders was so excited to find an invitation in the mailbox! But his heart sank when he opened the card and saw it was from Jason's father. The party was for Kevin's friend Jason.

"Is that a birthday invitation?" Mrs. Sanders asked, glancing at the card in his hand.

Kevin laid it facedown on the table.

"Some kids won't want to go," he explained.

"Why not?" asked his mother.

"Because the party is for Jason. His older brother, Michael, will be there and some of my friends don't like to be around him. They say he's retarded."

"No one should call Michael 'retarded.' He is mentally disabled," said Mother. "He had a high fever when he was a baby, and it made him a little different. That's all. But he is a sweet child."

"I know," said Kevin. "But he's not like everyone else—so there will be kids who won't want to go to the party. Maybe I shouldn't go either."

"Kevin Christopher Sanders, I'm surprised at you," his mother scolded. "How could you be so insensitive?"

Kevin looked down at the table. He knew that the only time his mother called him by his middle name was when she was upset.

"I'm sorry, Mom," he apologized. "It's just that I feel embarrassed around Michael. I've seen how he acts. He makes loud noises, he drops things, and he sometimes drools. He thinks it's fun to chase cats, too. Last week I saw Michael run right into the street to catch a kitten. He could have been hurt if his mother hadn't saved him."

Kevin's mom had a concerned look on her face. "There is something I want you to understand," she said. "All of us are different in one way or another, and no one is perfect. God made each person special. When a person is disabled like Michael, we must be very careful to protect his or her feelings and to show respect. Someday you or I may be disabled too. It is not right to act as if we are better than others or to hurt them in some way."

"I understand, Mom," said Kevin. "But what about Jason's party? What if no one goes?"

"You may be surprised to see how many are there. Why don't you talk to your father about all of this when he comes home?"

Eight-year-old Kevin pushed back his chair and sighed. "OK," he said. He picked up a bag of Ruffles potato chips and went into the living room. Clicking on the television remote, he sat down in his father's easy chair and stuffed three chips in his mouth. *Spider-Man* was on. It was one of his favorite shows, but Kevin wasn't paying attention.

What should I do? he thought. *Jason is my friend, and I really want to go to his party. I like Michael, too, even if he does strange things. But the party might not be much fun if a lot of the kids don't show up.*

Kevin clicked off the television remote and tossed it on the coffee table. He watched it slide to the edge where half of it hung over. He waited for it to fall, but it didn't.

I'll talk to Dad about this when he gets home, Kevin decided.

Finishing the last broken potato chip, he crumpled up the bag and threw it in the trash.

An hour later Kevin met his father at the door and began explaining the problem. Mr. Sanders listened while he hung up his coat and took off his tie. He sat down in the easy chair and took a deep breath.

"I talked to your mom on the phone earlier today, Kevin. I agree that it's important for you to go to the party. That's the best way to let Jason know you're his friend. It will let him know that you want to be friends with Michael, too."

"But Dad," said Kevin, "I don't know if the other kids will go."

"Well, let me just ask you this question. What would Jesus do in this situation? Why don't you ask him?"

Kevin rubbed his forehead and looked down at the ground. "I guess that's a good idea," he said. "Maybe I'll do that."

His father smiled and nodded his head. "I think that's the right thing to do," he said.

Time went by quickly, and before long the party was only a few days away. Kevin and his mother decided to go to Walgreen's to get a present. Mrs. Sanders pushed the cart down the aisle, pulling items she needed off the shelves. She looked at her list and finished crossing things off.

"Kevin, why don't you go to the toy section and pick out something for Jason?" she asked.

The boy's face lit up! Kevin always liked to have an excuse to look at toys.

He began to run toward aisle 14. When he got there, he saw so many fun things! Kevin checked out the cars, trucks, action figures, and model kits that lined the shelves in perfect order.

What would I want for a present if it were my birthday? Kevin thought.

Just then a familiar voice called his name. He turned to see Robert and Mark, two kids from his class, standing behind him.

"Hi, guys," said Kevin, smiling. "Are you going to Jason Mooney's party on Saturday?"

"No way!" said Robert. "His brother will be there. He does dumb things. He'll ruin the party."

"He's mentally disabled," said Kevin.

Robert said, "I don't care. I'm not going!"

"Neither am I," said Mark. "Anyone who would want to be around Michael is *un*cool—that's why none of our friends are going."

Kevin's face got hot. He began to see how unfair it was for kids to make fun of Michael. Suddenly, Kevin understood what his mother was saying. He also remembered his father's words, "What would Jesus do?"

"See you around," said Mark. He and Robert walked over to the magazine rack, where Robert's mother was standing. They began flipping through comic books.

Kevin felt a lump in his throat. He went on looking at the toys, but he couldn't concentrate. He pulled one of the boxes off the shelf and hurried back to his mother.

On the way home, Kevin talked about Robert and Mark and the mean things they had said about Michael.

"Do you know what, Mom?" he asked. "Those guys can say what they want, but I'm glad I decided to go to the party. I'm going to call Jason and help him think of some more kids to invite!"

Mrs. Sanders smiled. "Good idea," she said. "I think you're going to have a good time on Saturday."

"Me, too," said Kevin.

On the day of the party, Kevin helped his mother wrap Jason's present. Then they drove to the Mooneys' house. When Kevin knocked on the door, Michael answered it and immediately snatched the gift from Kevin's arms.

"For me?" he asked.

"For your brother," answered Kevin with a smile.

Jason joined them at the front door. "Hey, dude," he said. "Come in and check out the cake."

The boys headed into the dining room, where a large white box was sitting on the table. A lot of kids were standing around, waiting for the party to start. Jason proudly lifted the lid to display a cake with Star Wars decorations on the top.

"Wow!" said Kevin. "That's really cool."

Michael rushed over and stuck his finger in the icing, smearing the decoration.

"No, Michael!" scolded Jason. "The cake is for later."

The boy looked embarrassed as he put the frosting on his tongue.

Then Mrs. Mooney came into the room with four pizza boxes. "Are we ready to eat?" she asked.

Kevin glanced around the room. He saw some kids from church and school, and a few from around the neighborhood. In the corner of the room were some grown-ups, including two grandmothers with blue-and-silver hair.

Kevin tapped Jason on the shoulder and whispered in his ear. "You'd have had a full house if Robert, Mark, and their friends had come too," he said.

"You're right," Jason answered. "We sent invitations to all of them. But when we found out they weren't coming, my dad and I invited some other kids. By the way, thanks for helping us to come up with some names."

Kevin looked at the giant cake and the four pizza boxes on the table. He noticed

the balloons, streamers, and party decorations around the room, and all the bottles of soda on the counter. If the kids who had stayed away only knew what they were missing! It was going to be a great party.

Michael was pretty quiet throughout the meal. There were a few times when he tried to answer questions that were meant for someone else. Once he shouted at the top of his lungs when Jason tried to wipe his mouth. It made Kevin feel a little embarrassed, but he knew Michael couldn't help it. The real test came when Baxter, the Mooneys' cat, entered the room.

"Kitty cat!" Michael exclaimed. He jumped out of his chair and headed straight for the startled animal.

Michael chased the cat wherever he went, grabbing for his tail or leg.

Later that afternoon Mr. Mooney hung a Darth Vader piñata by the garage. The kids swung at it a number of times, trying to knock the candy out of it. But not Michael—he wanted to be with Baxter. He followed the cat up and down the stairs and around the backyard.

The other kids went on to play Pin the Tail on the Donkey, but Michael still stayed with the cat. He sat on the patio and stroked Baxter's fur with his fingers.

Later that afternoon Mrs. Mooney called everyone inside to watch Jason open his presents. They sat in a circle as Michael helped him rip the paper off the boxes.

Kevin reached over and handed Michael the gift he had brought. "Open this one for Jason," he said.

Michael tore the Snoopy paper off and looked at the front of the box. "It's a water rocket!" said Kevin. He leaned close to Michael so he could explain how it operated. "This is a fun toy," said Kevin. "You fill it with water and pump it; then it shoots up in the air!"

Michael laughed and clapped his hands. He seemed to really like the gift Kevin had given his brother.

When the last present was opened, Michael picked up the rocket and took Kevin by the hand. "Come outside," he said. "Show me!"

Kevin gave Jason a questioning look. "It's OK," said Jason. "Go ahead."

Everyone followed them outside to watch the excitement. Kevin set up the toy on the pavement and did all the steps carefully. Then he shot the rocket 20 feet into the air!

"Look at it go!" shouted Jason.

Michael giggled and jumped up and down on the pavement. He seemed to have forgotten all about Baxter for the moment. When the rocket hit the ground, Michael ran to retrieve it and put it on the launching pad again.

Kevin was having as much fun watching Michael as he was playing with the toy. As the rocket went up for the second time, Michael grinned and shouted and stomped his feet on the ground. Just because Michael was mentally disabled, it didn't mean he wasn't fun to be around. In fact, it was quite the opposite!

When the party was over, Jason and Kevin walked to the street curb to wait for Kevin's mother.

"Thanks for inviting me," said Kevin. "I had a great time."

"Thanks for coming," said Jason. "Some kids don't want to be around my brother because he's different. I'm glad you didn't feel that way." Kevin smiled at his friend as his mom's Ford pulled up to the curb.

On the way home Kevin told his mother all about the party and how much fun it was. The snobby kids from school had missed out on a good time! But then again, they didn't deserve to be there anyway.

Kevin thought about his friend and realized how much Jason loved his brother. Kevin was proud of himself for choosing to come to the party—one of the best decisions he had ever made!

The Parable of the Wedding Banquet

MATTHEW 22:1-14

Jesus told a story about a king who instructed his servants to invite many important people to a wedding ceremony. His son was being honored, and the father wanted everything to be special. Wonderful food was prepared, and all the plans had been made. But those who were to be the guests were very rude. They wouldn't come to the ceremony. They were even unkind to the servants who invited them, going about their business as usual.

The king became very angry and told the servants to get rid of those people. Then he asked his workers to go into the streets and invite anyone who wanted to come. The wedding hall was filled with these other guests, and it was a wonderful feast. But during this banquet, the king saw a man who was not wearing wedding clothes. That man had not been invited, so the servants threw him out.

The meaning of this parable is very important. God is the king in the story. He is planning a wonderful event in heaven. Jesus Christ is the Son, who will be honored throughout eternity. Those of us who accept the invitation will be with the Son in heaven forever and ever. But the man who crashed the party without wedding clothes is like a person whose sins haven't been forgiven. He will not be permitted in heaven after he dies.

Jason's party was much smaller than the wedding banquet in heaven that Jesus told about. But Jason's party was like that big banquet because he had friends who didn't want to come. Some of Jason's friends were unkind to his brother, Michael, who was mentally handicapped. These rude friends were like the first guests in Jesus' story—the guests who wouldn't come to the king's banquet. Even Jason's friend Kevin wasn't sure at first if he should accept the invitation because he thought Michael was odd. But Kevin changed his mind and decided he really wanted to be at the party. He also helped Jason think of more kids who might come.

Like the king in Jesus' story, Jason's father did ask others to come to his son's party. He invited boys and girls who *wanted* to be there. The nice people who came to the party had a wonderful time. Michael made it fun for everyone.

When you're invited to a party, are you happy to go? Did you know that God has given you an invitation to Jesus' big banquet in heaven? Think about what you can do right now to get ready for that big party, where there will be many children and grown-ups from all over the world. The most special person there will be God's own Son, Jesus!

JCD